BIG-NOTE PIANO

A CHRISTMAS COLLECTION

ISBN-13: 978-0-7935-3421-0
ISBN-10: 0-7935-3421-6

HAL•LEONARD® CORPORATION

7777 W. BLUEMOUND RD. P.O. BOX 13819 MILWAUKEE, WI 53213

Visit Hal Leonard Online at
www.halleonard.com

A CHRISTMAS COLLECTION
2ND EDITION

CONTENTS

BECAUSE IT'S CHRISTMAS

(For All the Children)

Music by BARRY MANILOW
Lyric by BRUCE SUSSMAN and JACK FELDMAN

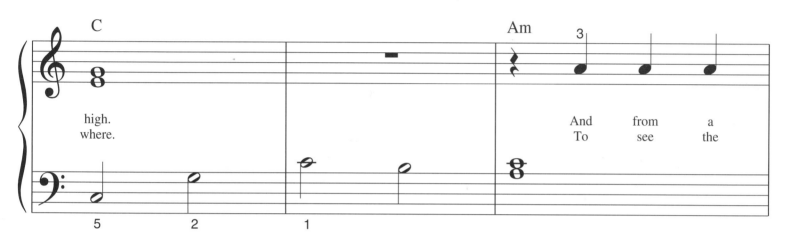

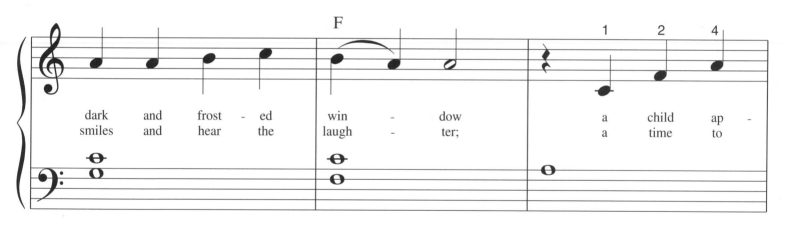

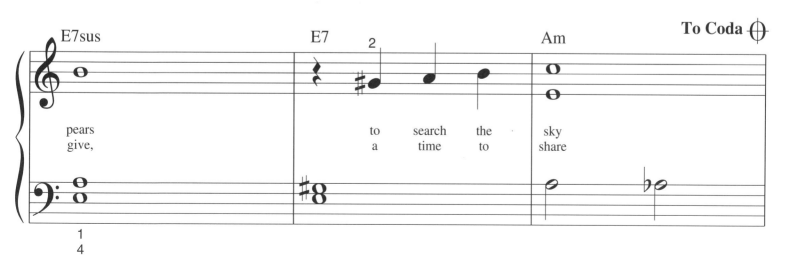

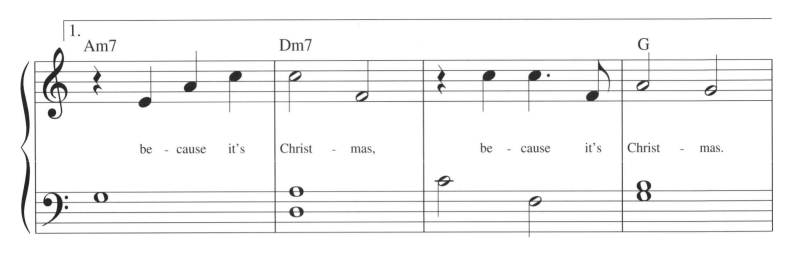

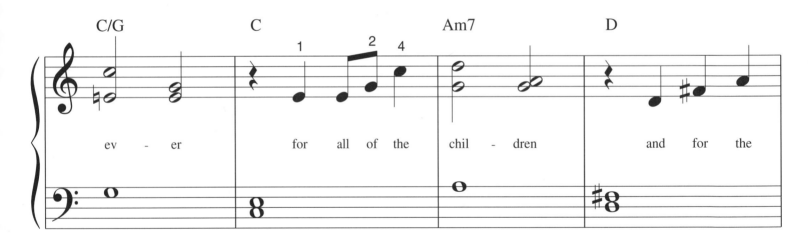

D.S. al Coda

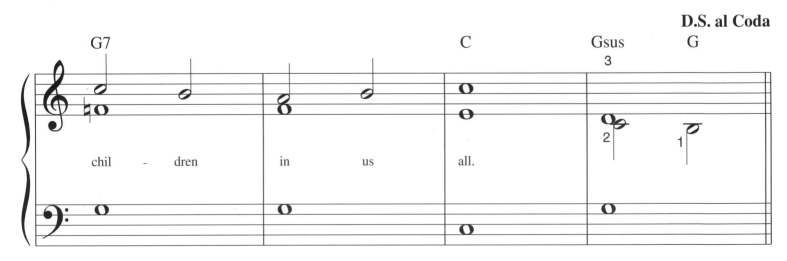

7

CODA

BLUE CHRISTMAS

Words and Music by BILLY HAYES
and JAY JOHNSON

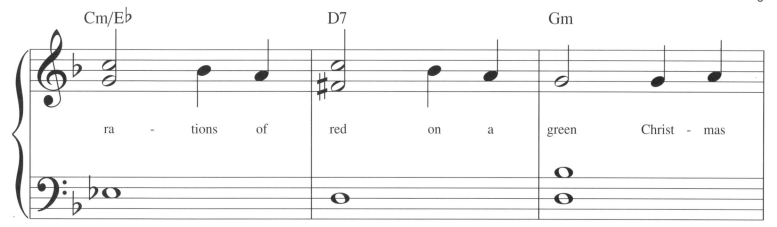

ra - tions of red on a green Christ - mas

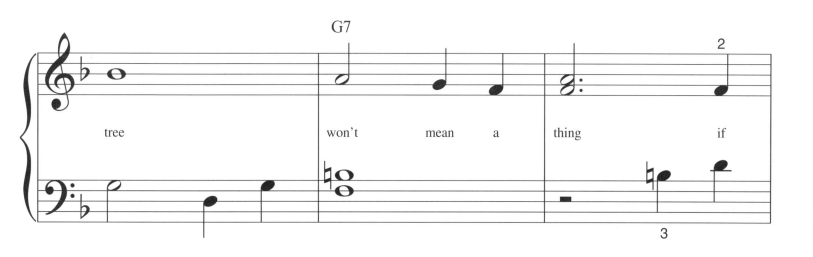

tree won't mean a thing if

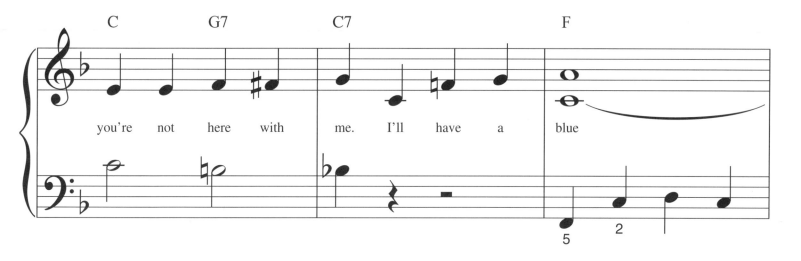

you're not here with me. I'll have a blue

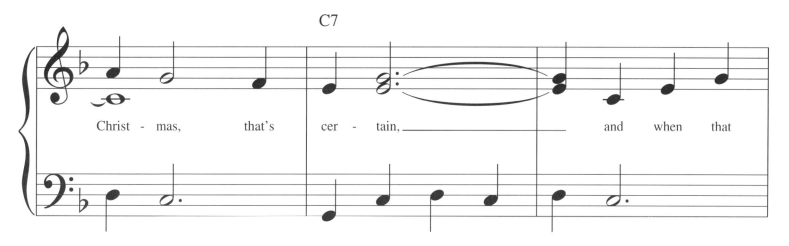

Christ - mas, that's cer - tain, and when that

CHRISTMAS IS

Lyrics by SPENCE MAXWELL
Music by PERCY FAITH

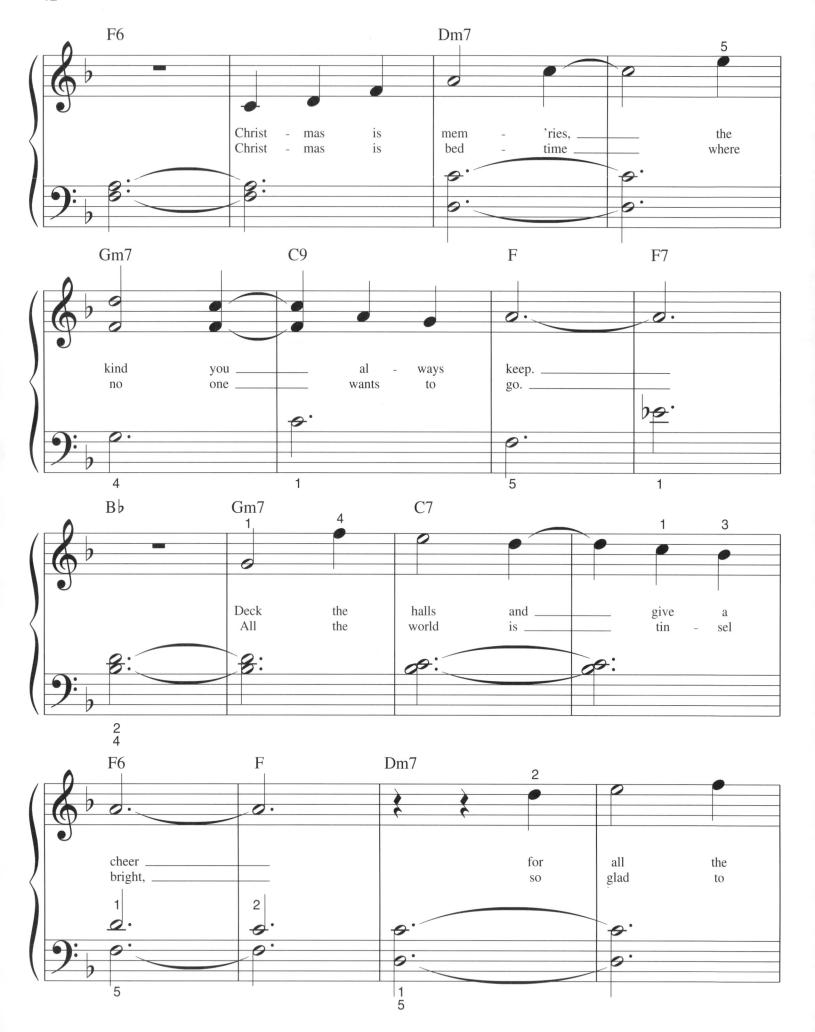

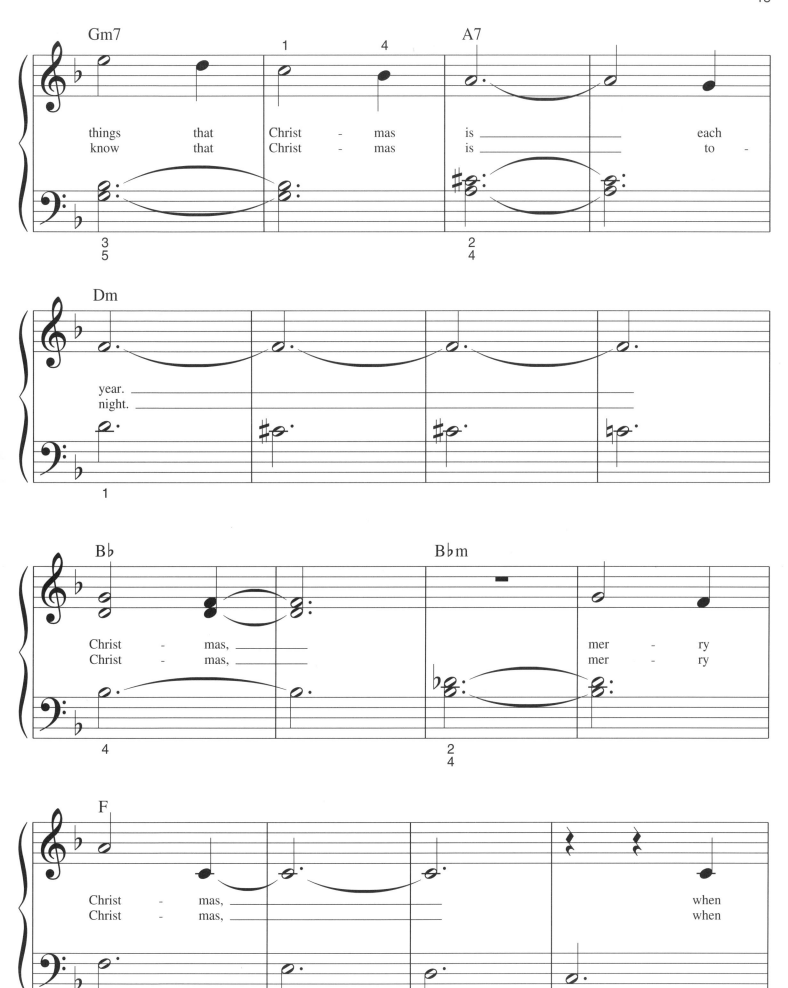

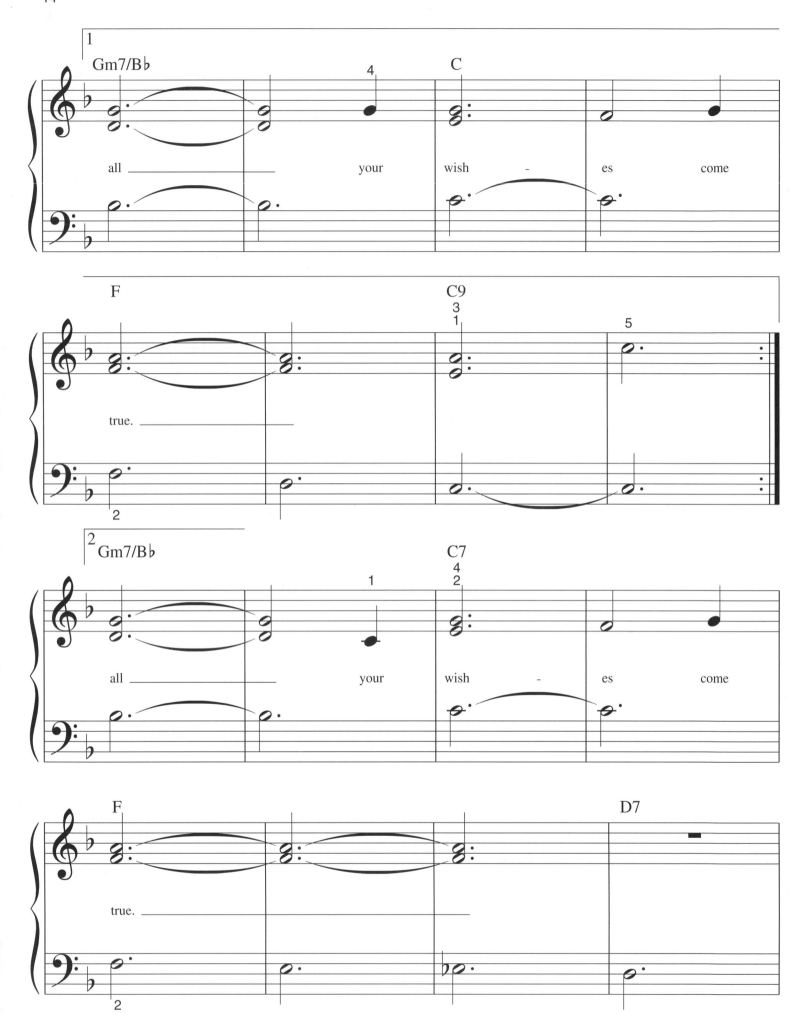

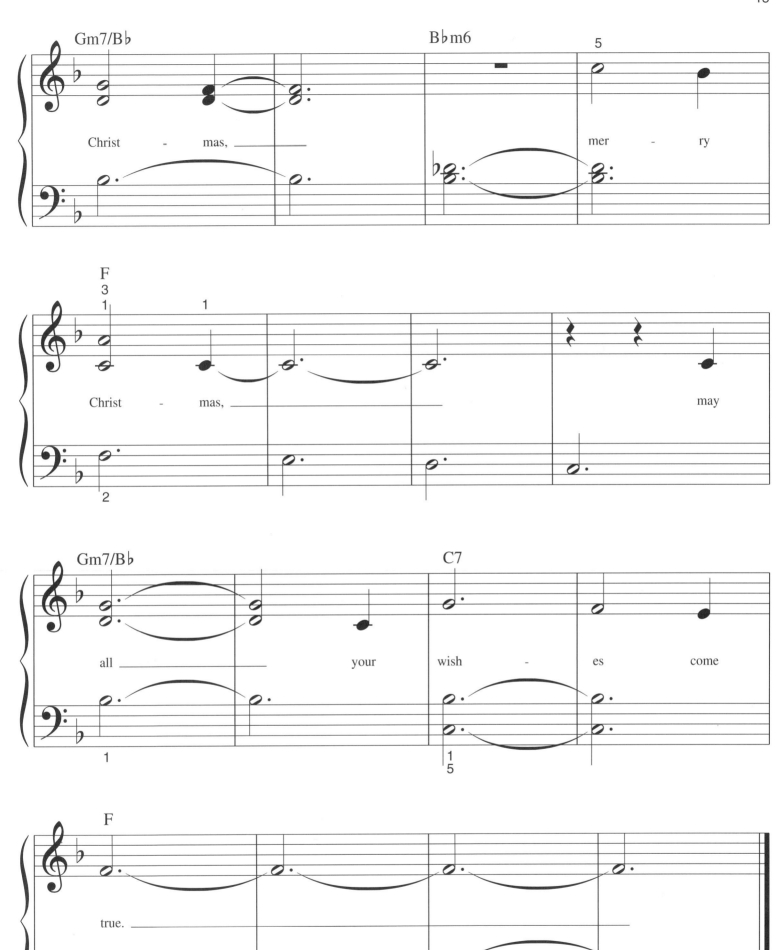

THE CHIPMUNK SONG

Words and Music by
ROSS BAGDASARIAN

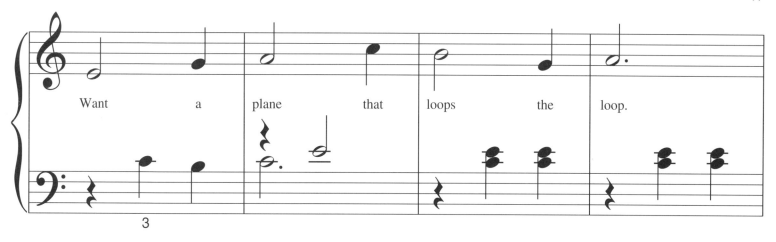

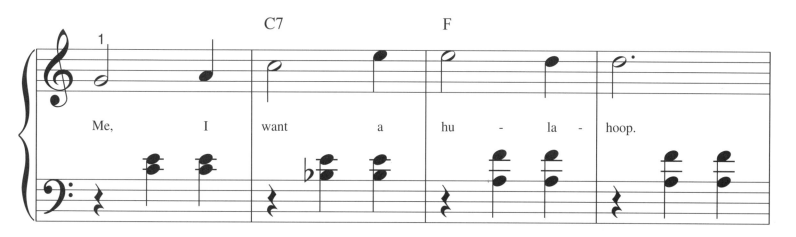

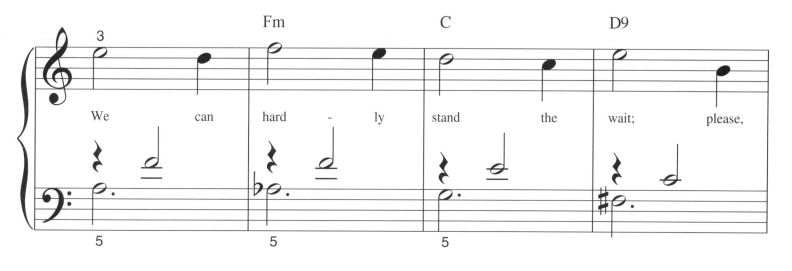

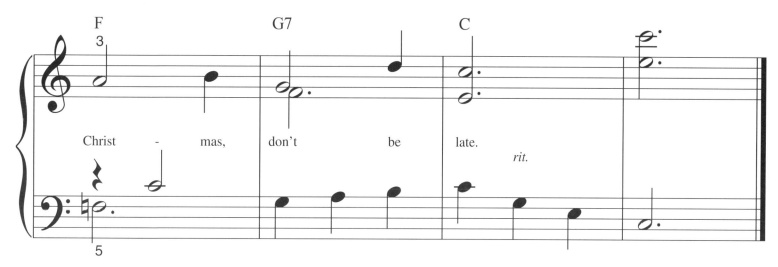

CHRISTMAS IS A-COMIN'
(May God Bless You)

Words and Music by
FRANK LUTHER

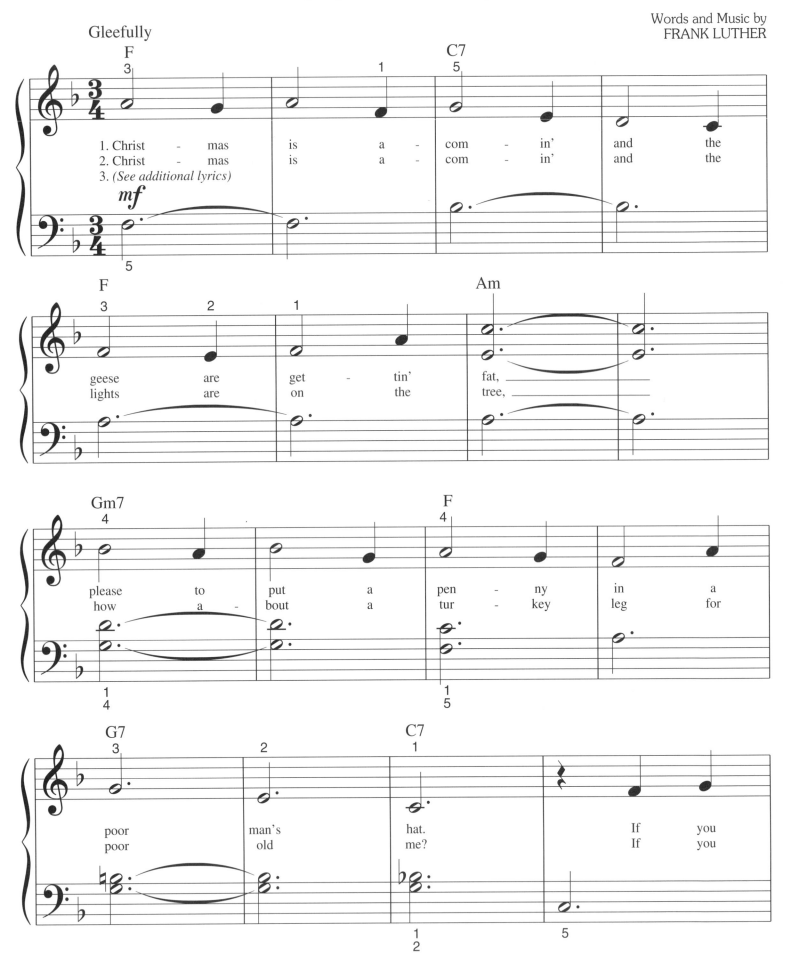

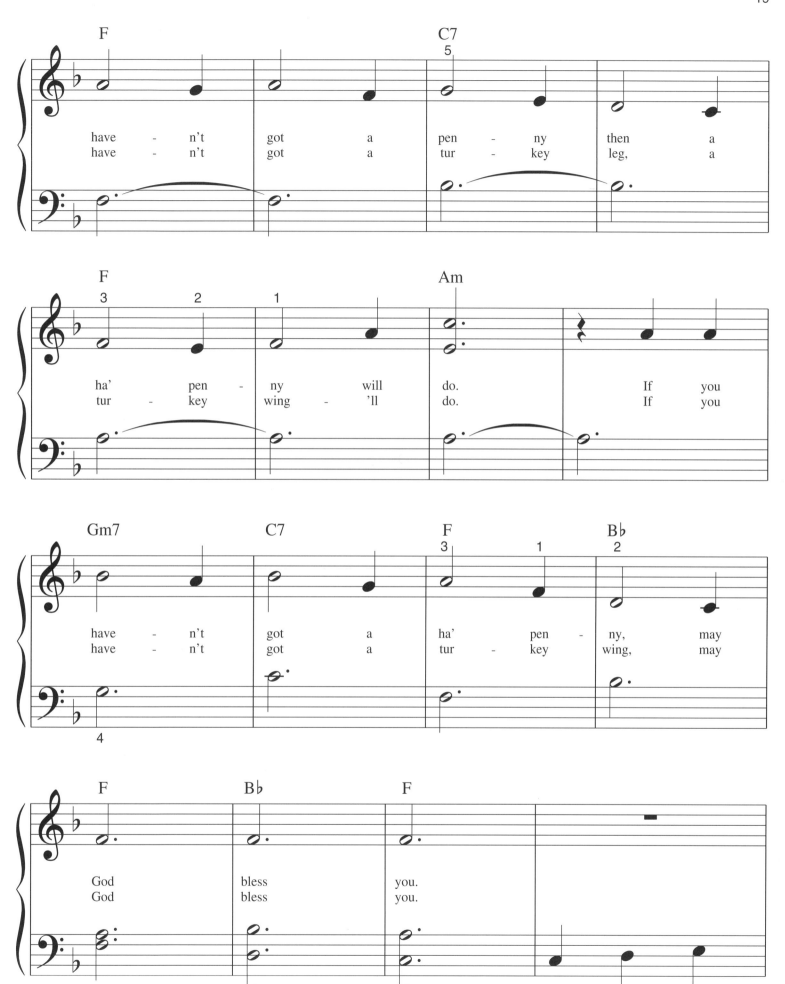

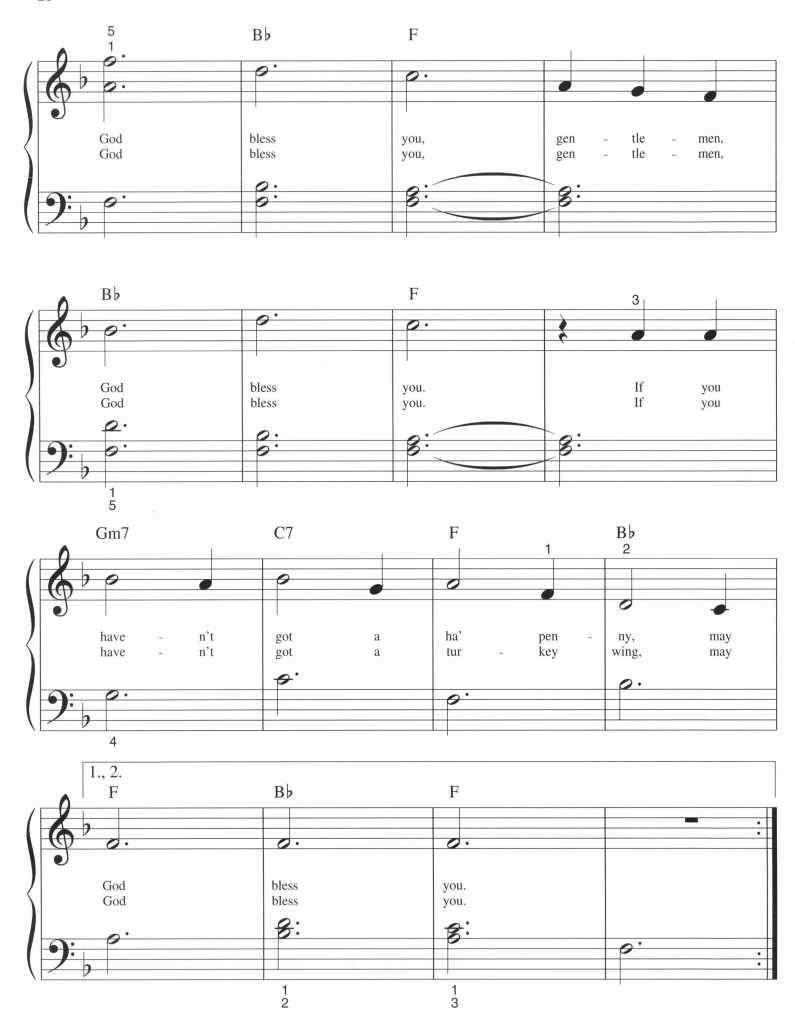

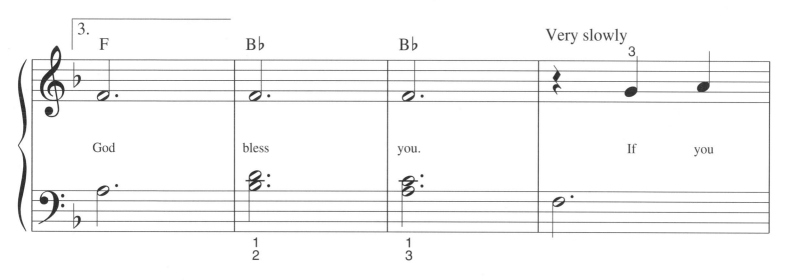

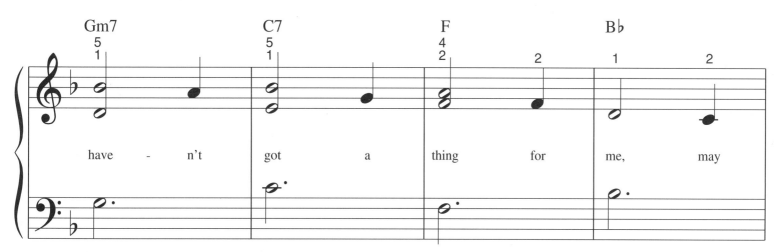

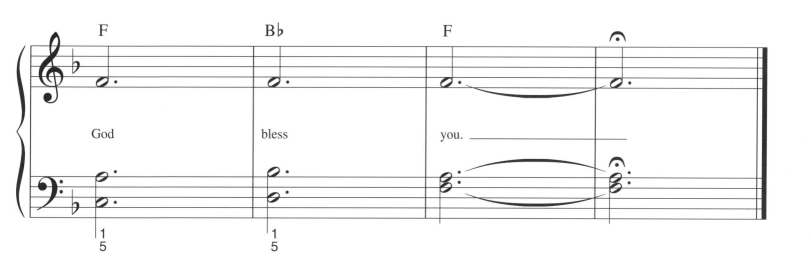

Additional Lyrics

3. Christmas is a-comin' and the egg is in the nog,
   Please to let me sit around your old Yule log.
   If you'd rather I didn't sit around, to stand around'll do.
   If you'd rather I didn't stand around, may God bless you.
   God bless you, gentlemen, God bless you.
   If you'd rather I didn't stand around, may God bless you.

THE CHRISTMAS SONG
(Chestnuts Roasting on an Open Fire)

Music and Lyric by MEL TORME
and ROBERT WELLS

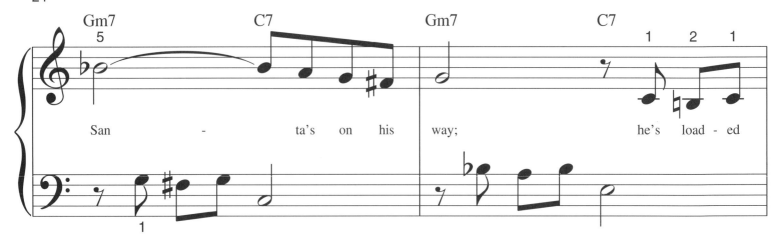

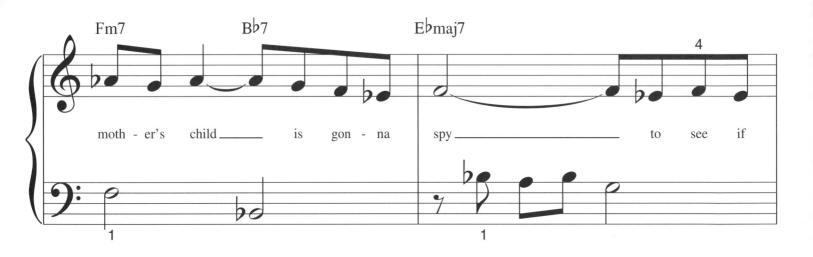

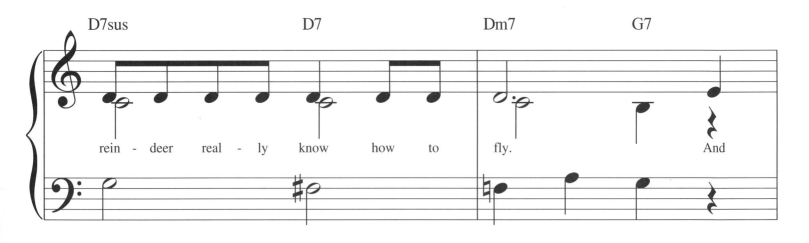

THE CHRISTMAS WALTZ

Words by SAMMY CAHN
Music by JULE STYNE

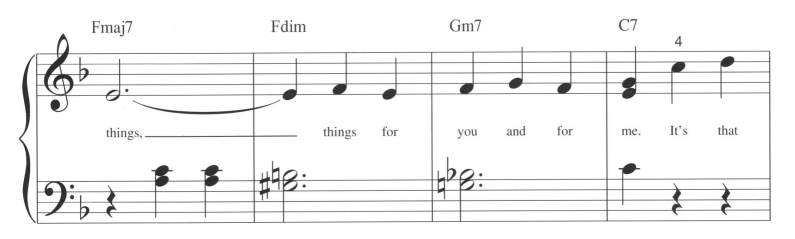

28

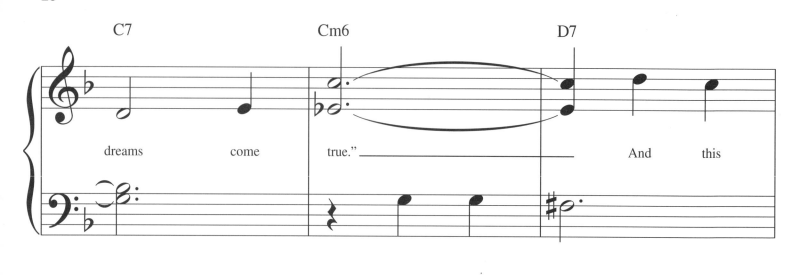

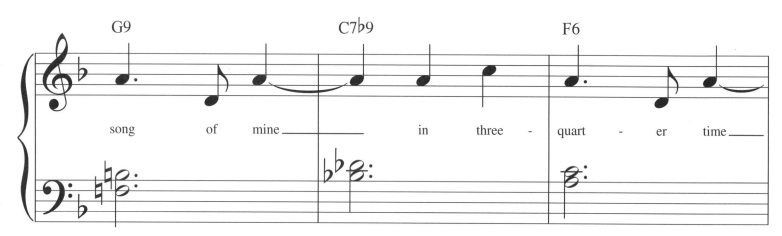

FROSTY THE SNOW MAN

Words and Music by STEVE NELSON
and JACK ROLLINS

31

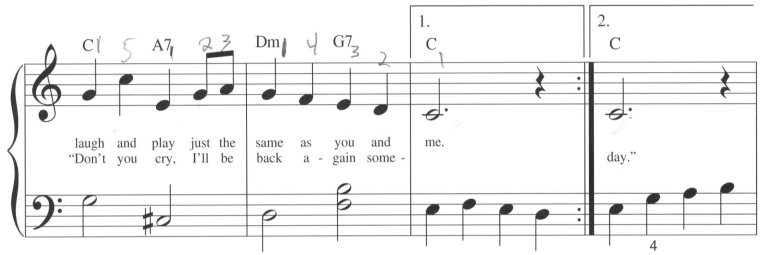

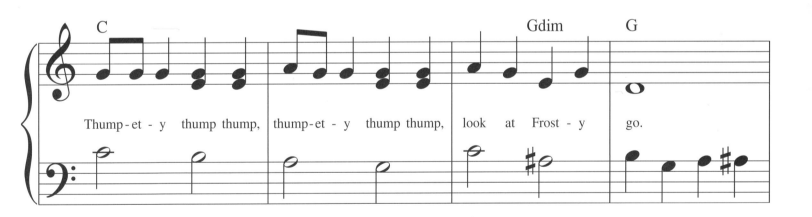

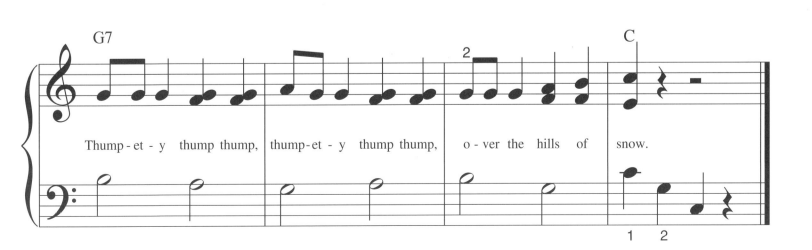

HAPPY HOLIDAY
from the Motion Picture Irving Berlin's HOLIDAY INN

Words and Music by
IRVING BERLIN

HERE COMES SANTA CLAUS
(Right Down Santa Claus Lane)

Words and Music by GENE AUTRY
and OAKLEY HALDEMAN

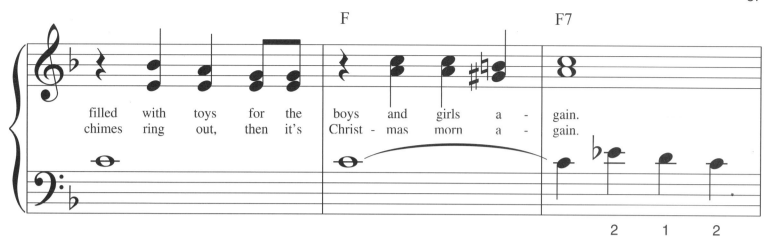

filled with toys for the boys and girls a - gain.
chimes ring out, then it's Christ - mas morn a - gain.

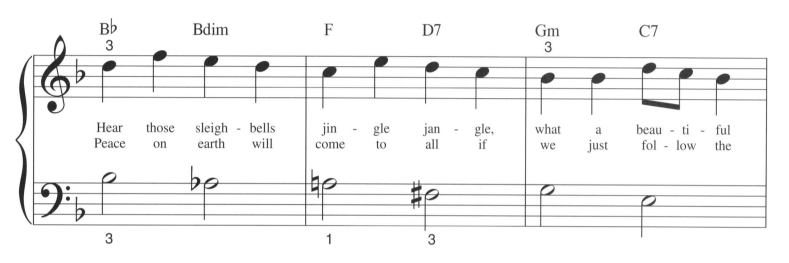

Hear those sleigh - bells jin - gle jan - gle, what a beau - ti - ful
Peace on earth will come to all if we just fol - low the

sight. Jump in bed, cov - er up your head, 'cause
light. Let's give thanks to the Lord a - bove, 'cause

San - ta Claus comes to - night.
San - ta Claus comes to - night.

A HOLLY JOLLY CHRISTMAS

Music and Lyrics by
JOHNNY MARKS

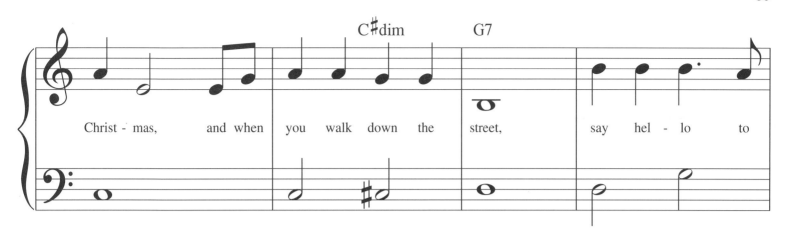

Christ - mas, and when you walk down the street, say hel - lo to

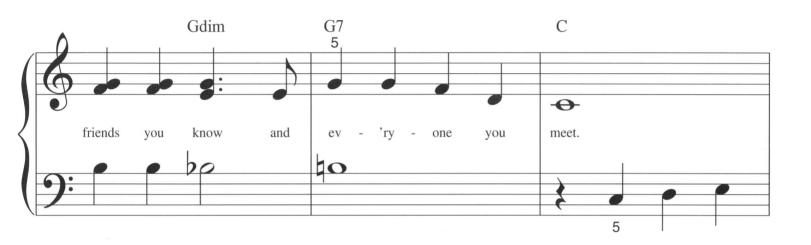

friends you know and ev - 'ry - one you meet.

Oh, ho, the mis - tle - toe hung where you can see.

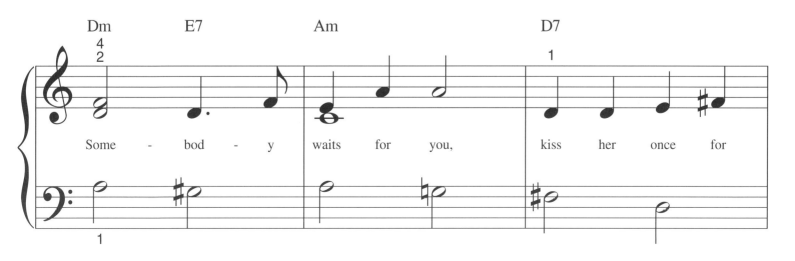

Some - bod - y waits for you, kiss her once for

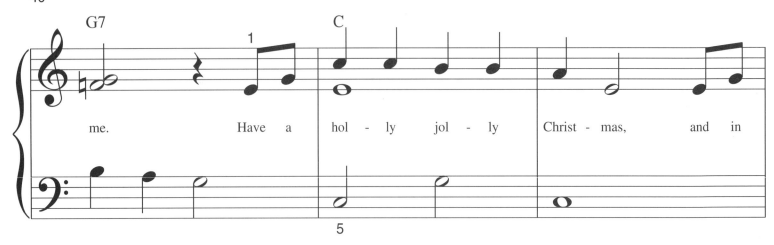

me. Have a hol - ly jol - ly Christ - mas, and in

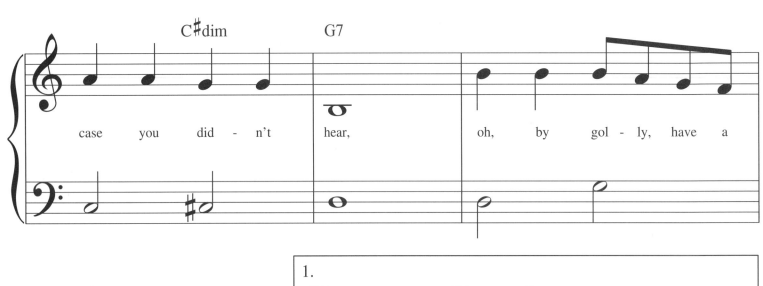

case you did - n't hear, oh, by gol - ly, have a

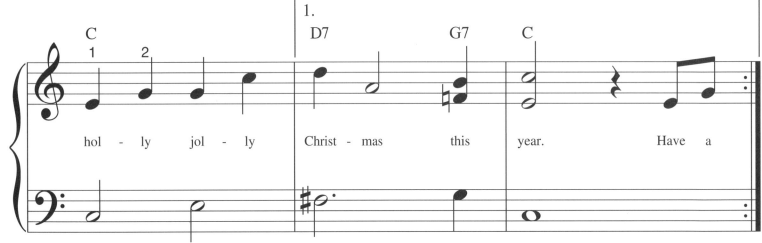

hol - ly jol - ly Christ - mas this year. Have a

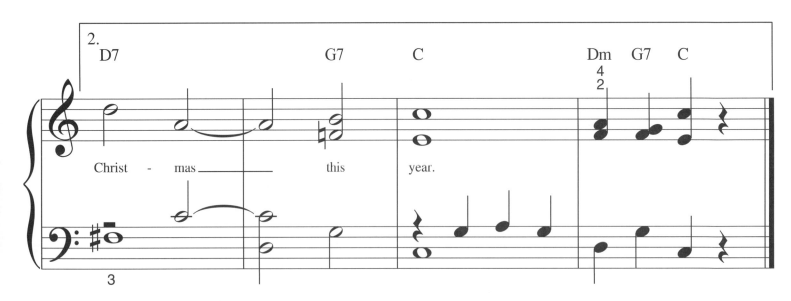

Christ - mas _____ this year.

I'LL BE HOME FOR CHRISTMAS

Words and Music by KIM GANNON
and WALTER KENT

Slowly, in 2

N.C.

mf

With pedal

F

G9

C

I'll   be

Cdim

home   for

Dm

Christ -   mas. _____

G7

Am

You   can

A7♭9

count   on   me. _____

Dm

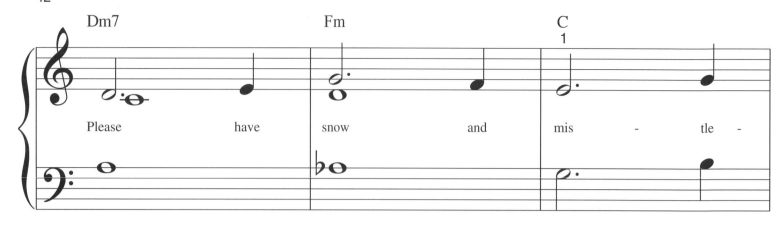

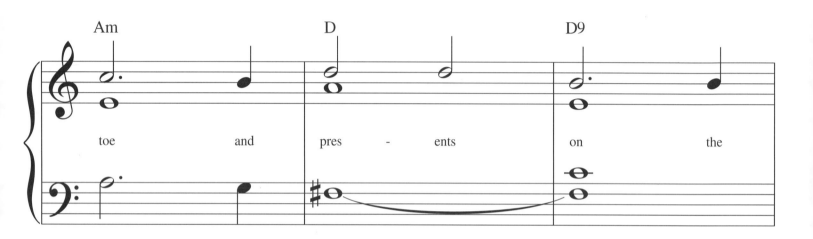

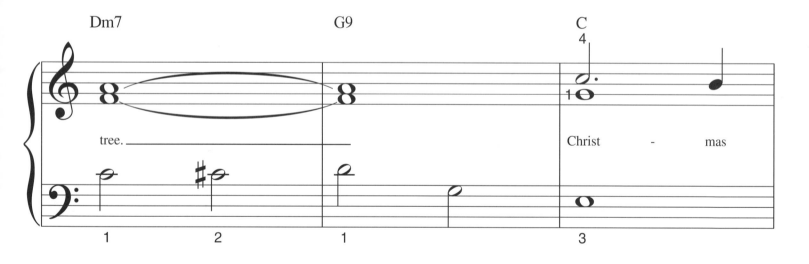

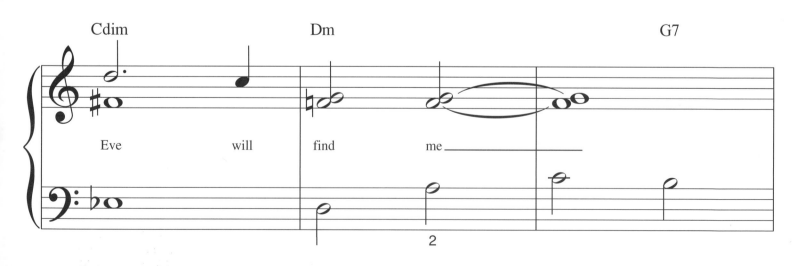

(There's No Place Like)
HOME FOR THE HOLIDAYS

Words by AL STILLMAN
Music by ROBERT ALLEN

I HEARD THE BELLS ON CHRISTMAS DAY

Words by HENRY WADSWORTH LONGFELLOW
Adapted by JOHNNY MARKS
Music by JOHNNY MARKS

I SAW MOMMY KISSING SANTA CLAUS

Words and Music by
TOMMIE CONNOR

IT'S BEGINNING TO LOOK LIKE CHRISTMAS

By MEREDITH WILLSON

Moderately, with a lilt

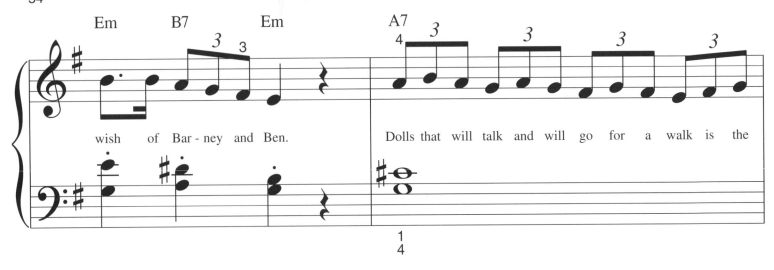

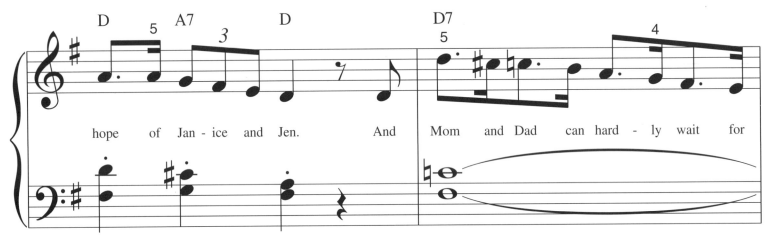

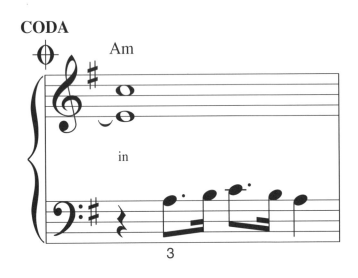

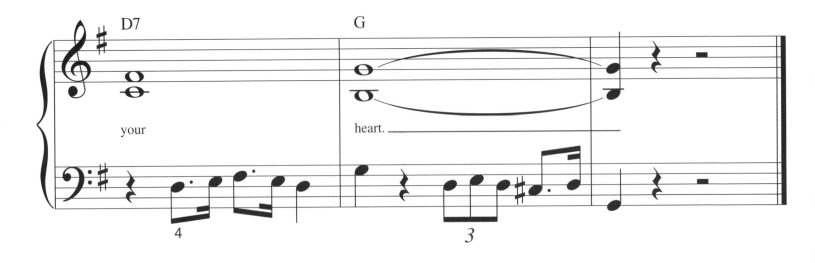

JINGLE-BELL ROCK

Words and Music by JOE BEAL
and JIM BOOTHE

jin - gle bells chime in jin - gle-bell time. Danc - in' and pranc - in' in

Jin - gle-bell Square in the frost - y air. What a

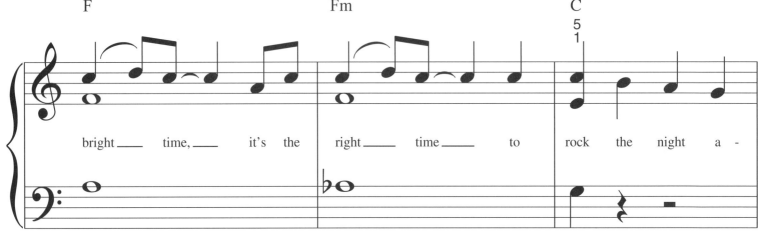

bright ___ time, ___ it's the right ___ time ___ to rock the night a -

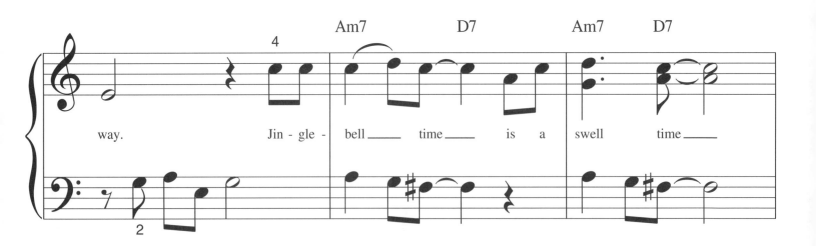

way. Jin - gle - bell ___ time ___ is a swell time ___

JINGLE, JINGLE, JINGLE

Music and Lyrics by
JOHNNY MARKS

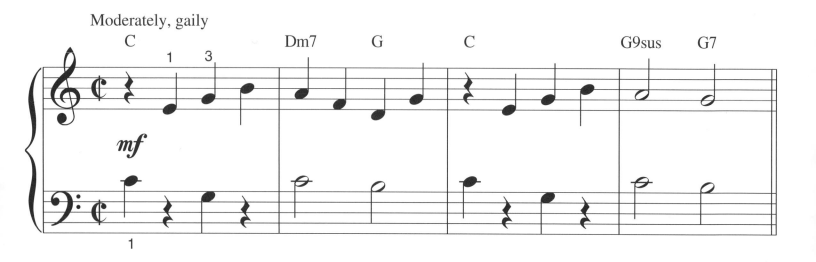

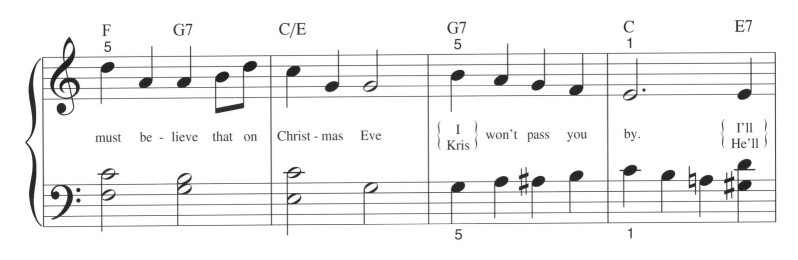

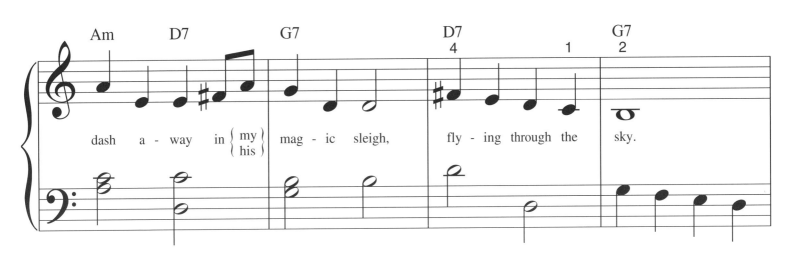

LET IT SNOW! LET IT SNOW! LET IT SNOW!

Words by SAMMY CAHN
Music by JULE STYNE

LET'S HAVE AN OLD FASHIONED CHRISTMAS

Lyric by LARRY CONLEY
Music by JOE SOLOMON

A MARSHMALLOW WORLD

Words by CARL SIGMAN
Music by PETER DE ROSE

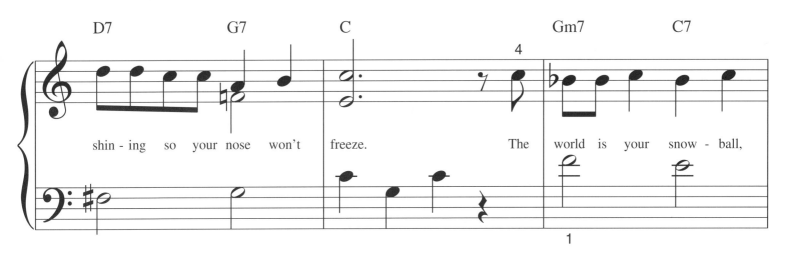

LITTLE SAINT NICK

Words and Music by BRIAN WILSON
and MIKE LOVE

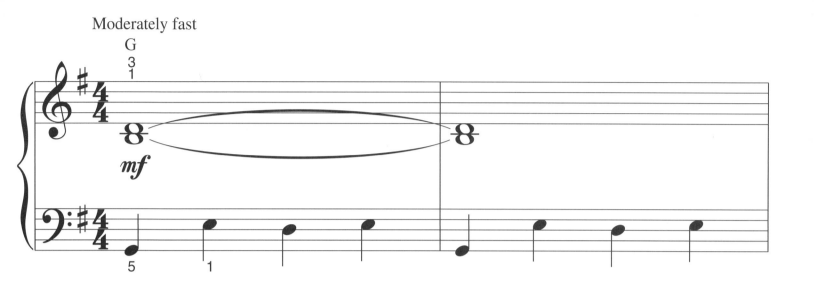

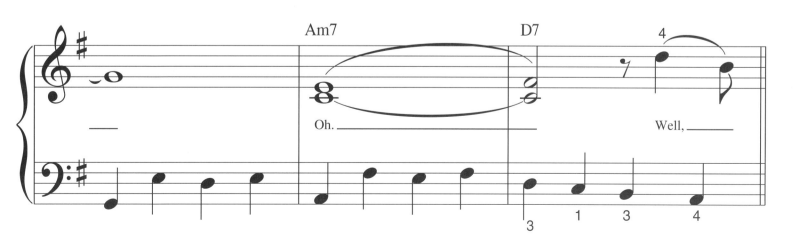

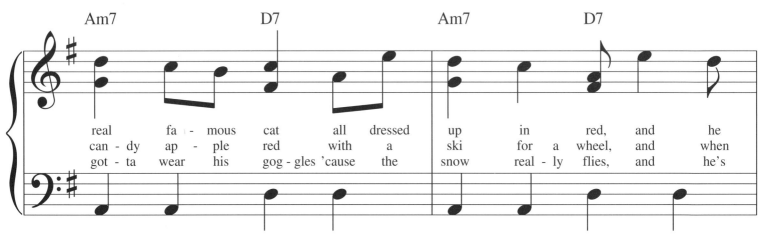

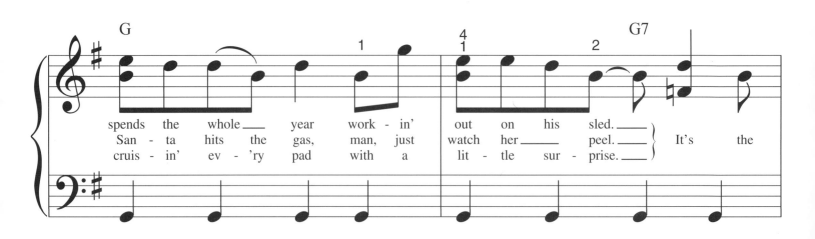

Run, run, rein - deer. He don't miss no one. And

Lit - tle Saint Nick. (Lit - tle Saint Nick.) Ah,

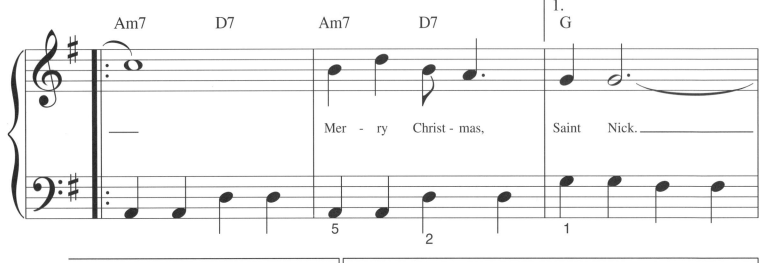

Mer - ry Christ - mas, Saint Nick.

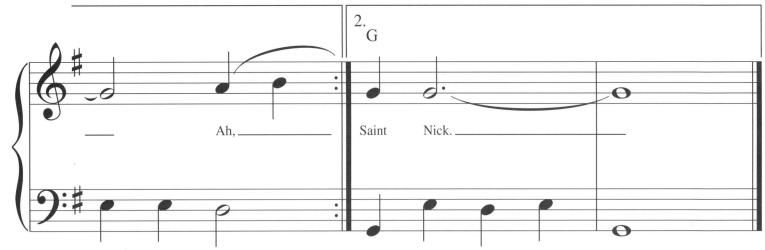

Ah, Saint Nick.

MISTER SANTA

Words and Music by
PAT BALLARD

Brightly, in 2

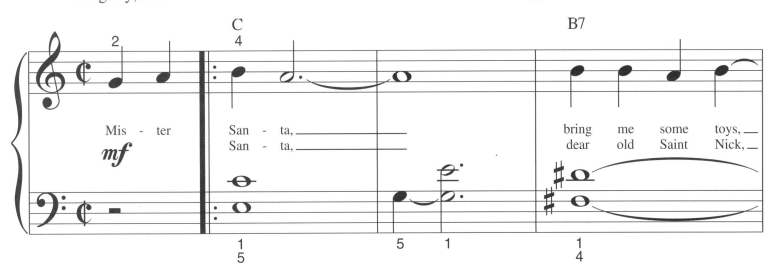

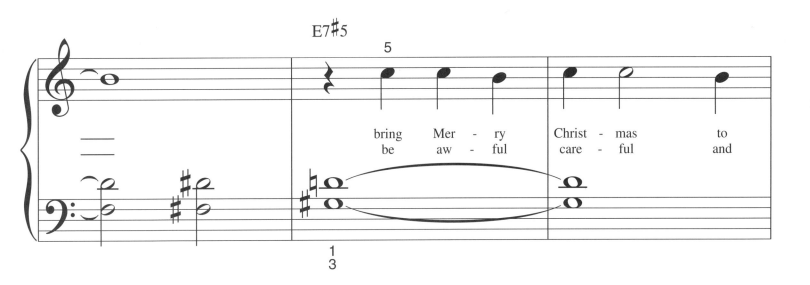

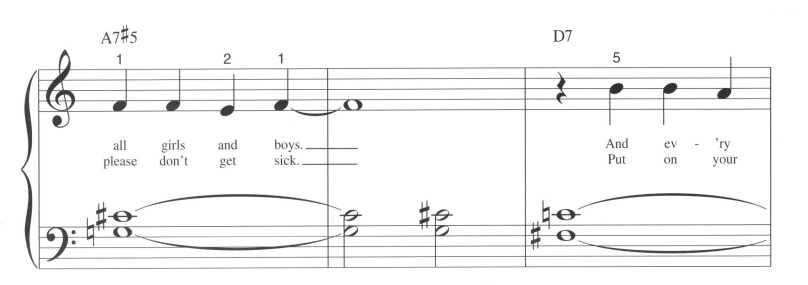

74

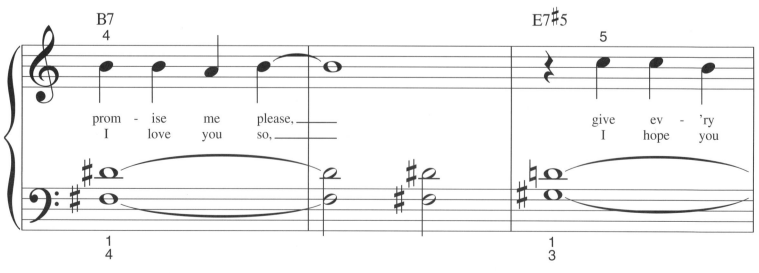

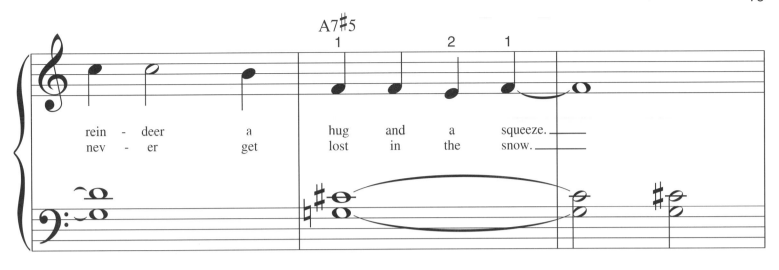

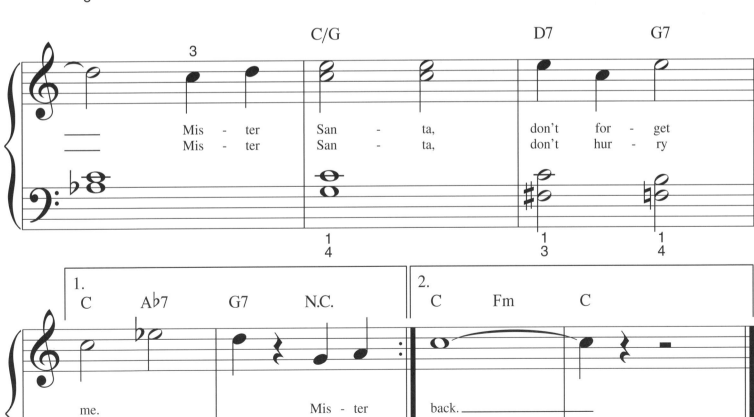

MISTLETOE AND HOLLY

Words and Music by FRANK SINATRA,
DOK STANFORD and HENRY W. SANICOLA

Oh by gosh, by gol - ly, it's time for
Oh by gosh, by jin - gle, it's time for
Oh by gosh, by gol - ly, it's time for

mis - tle - toe and hol - ly
car - ols and Kris Krin - gle.
mis - tle - toe and hol - ly.

To Coda

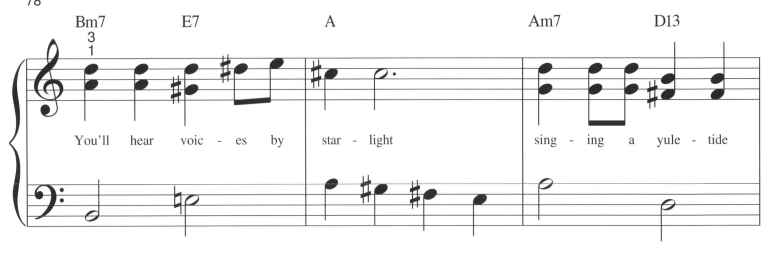

You'll hear voic - es by star - light   sing - ing a yule - tide

hymn.   **D.S. al Coda**   **CODA**   folks steal - in' a kiss or

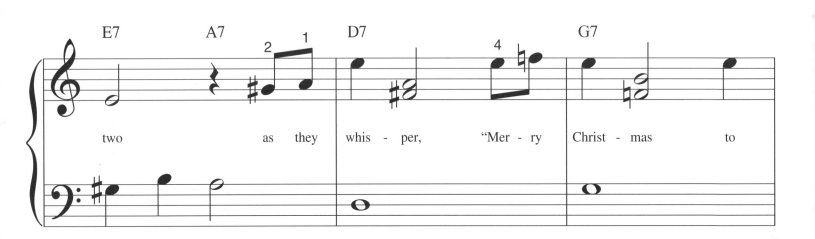

two   as they whis - per, "Mer - ry Christ - mas to

you."

NUTTIN' FOR CHRISTMAS

Words and Music by ROY BENNETT
and SID TEPPER

THE MOST WONDERFUL DAY OF THE YEAR

Music and Lyrics by
JOHNNY MARKS

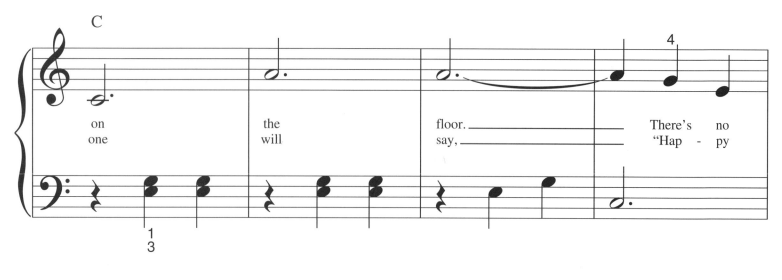

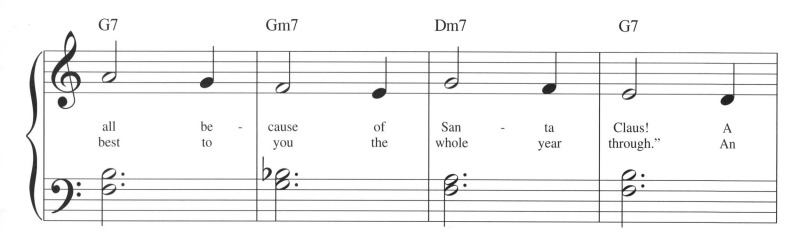

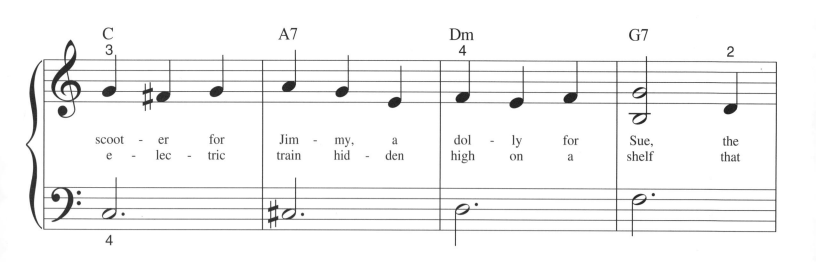

THE MOST WONDERFUL TIME OF THE YEAR

Words and Music by EDDIE POLA
and GEORGE WYLE

Brightly, in one

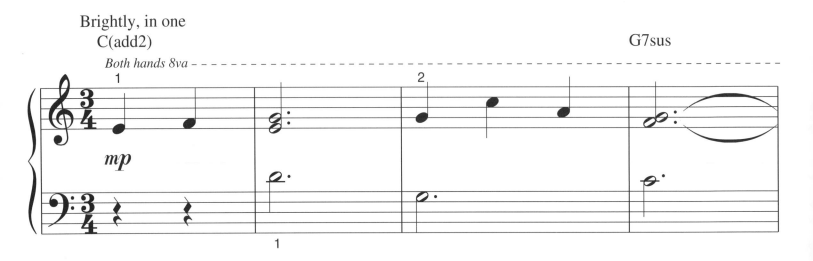

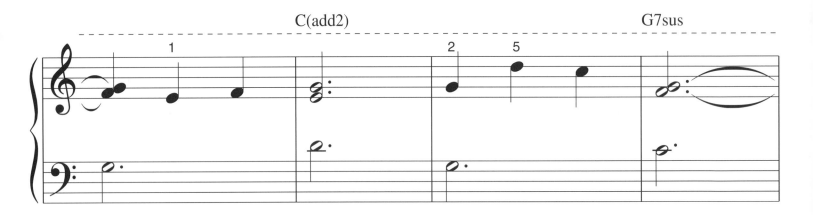

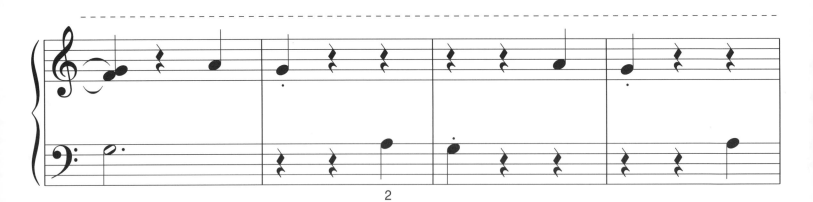

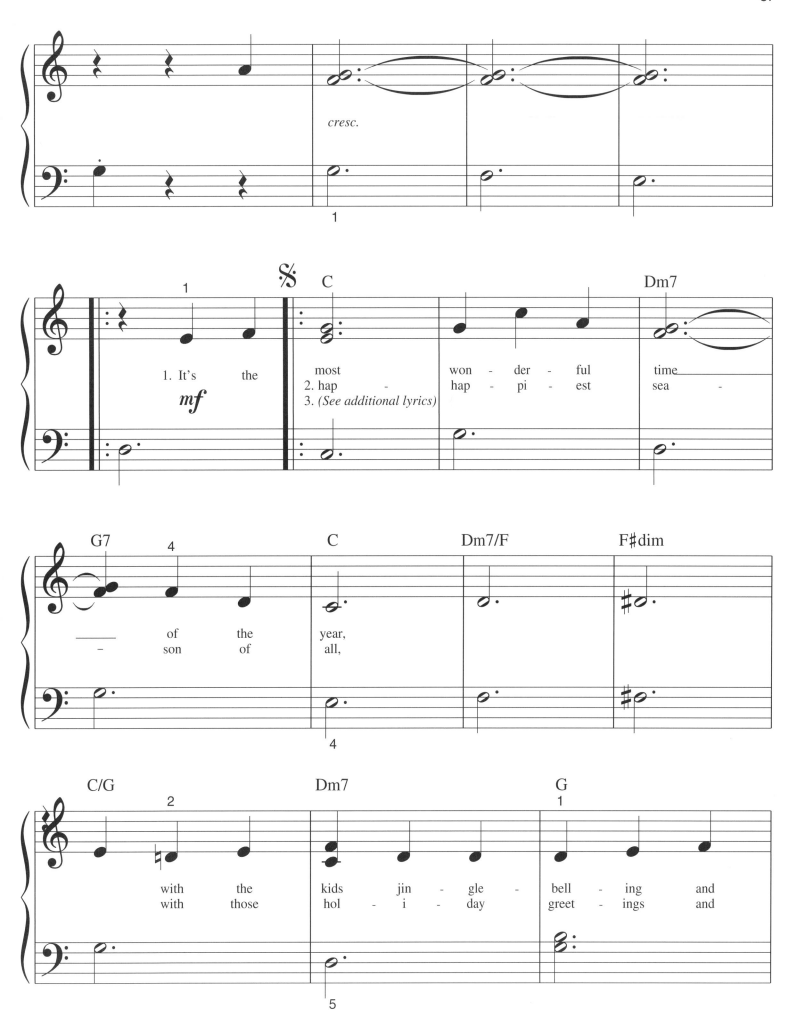

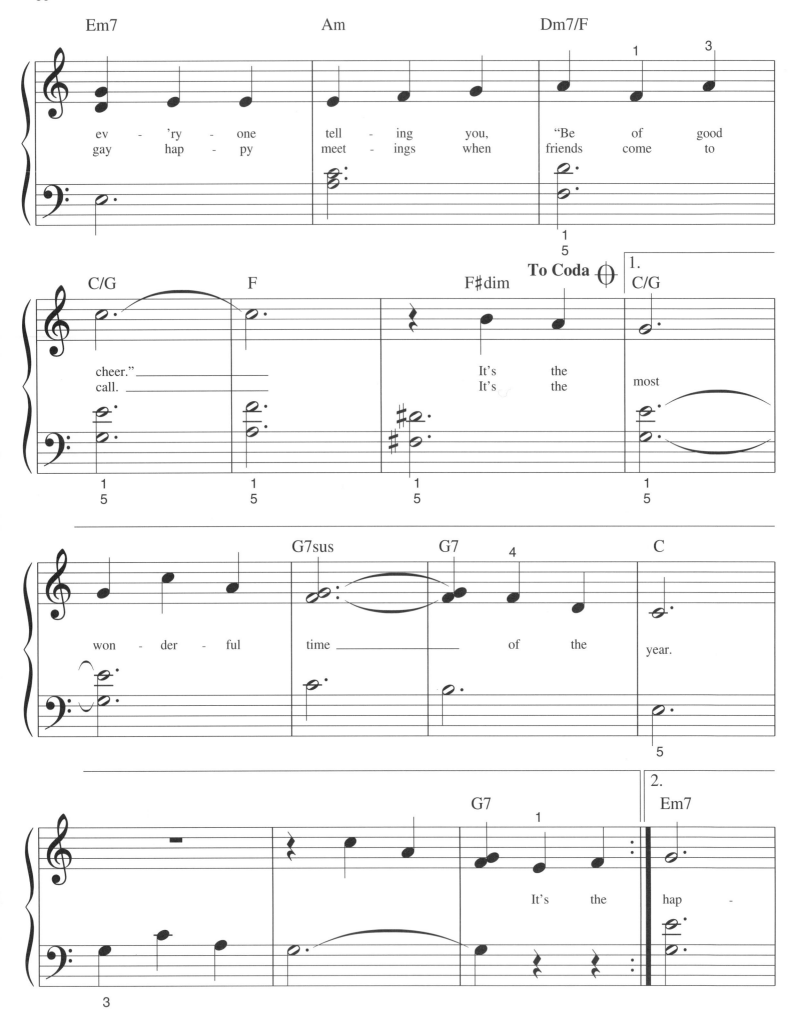

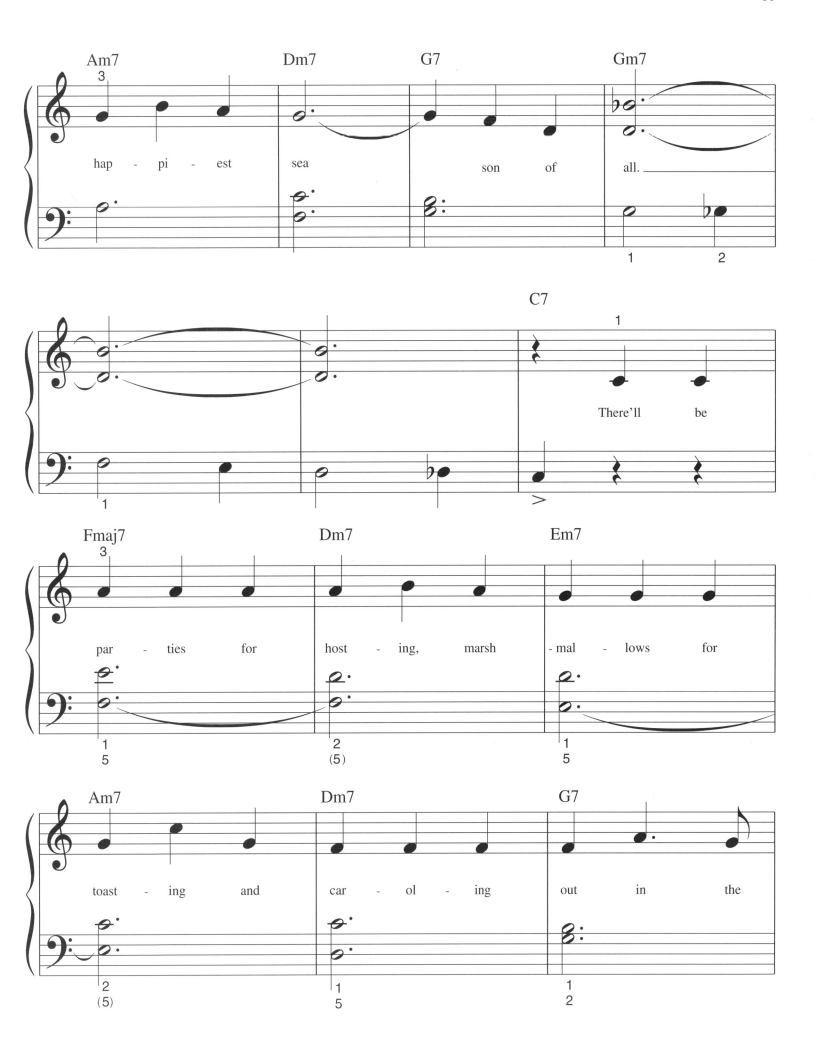

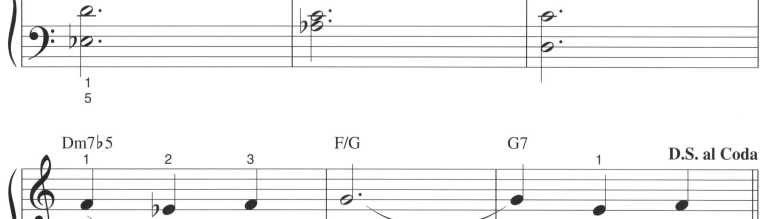

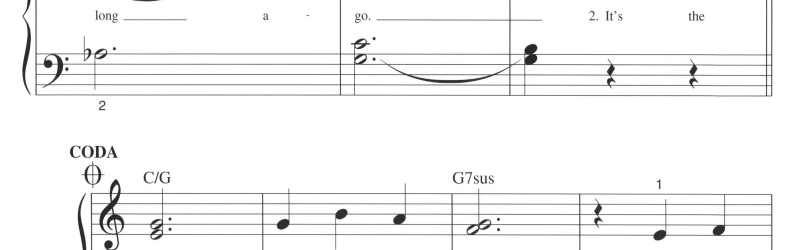

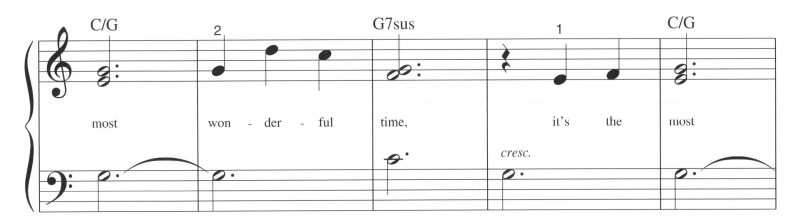

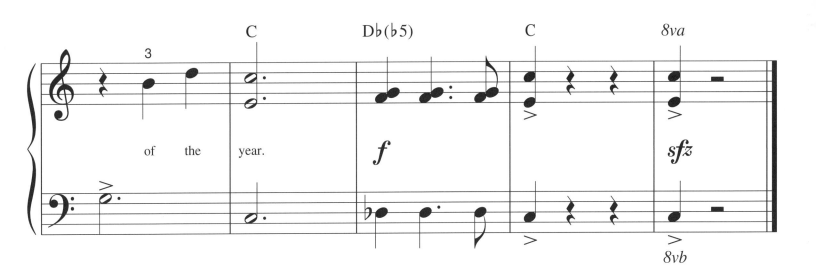

Additional Lyrics

3. It's the most wonderful time of the year.
    There'll be much mistletoeing and hearts will be glowing
        when loved ones are near.
    It's the most wonderful time,
    It's the most wonderful time,
    It's the most wonderful time of the year.

THE NIGHT BEFORE CHRISTMAS SONG

Music by JOHNNY MARKS
Lyrics adapted by JOHNNY MARKS
from Clement Moore's Poem

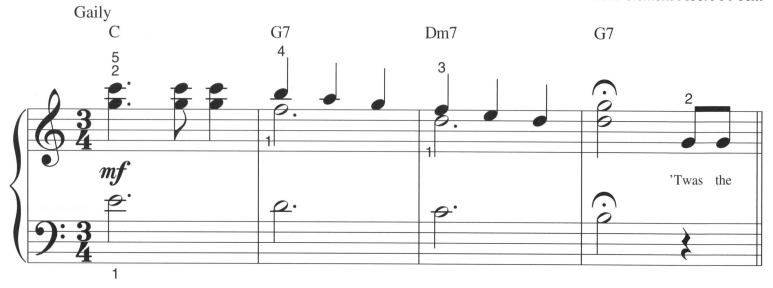

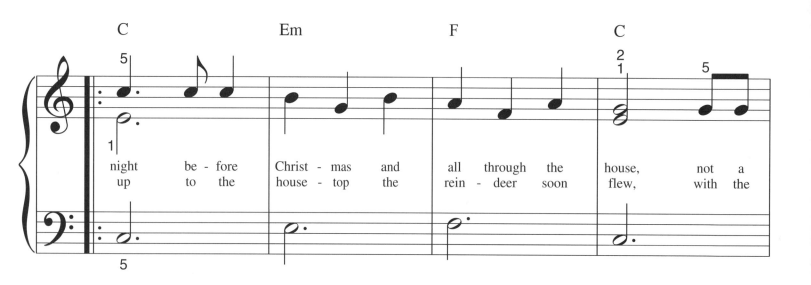

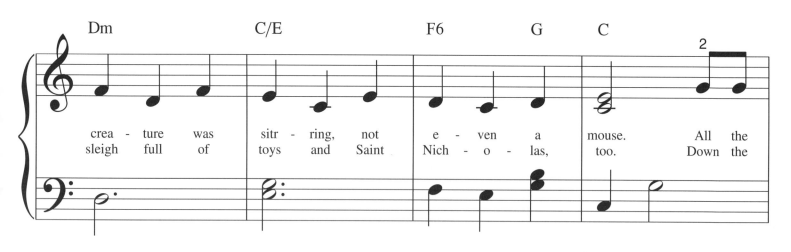

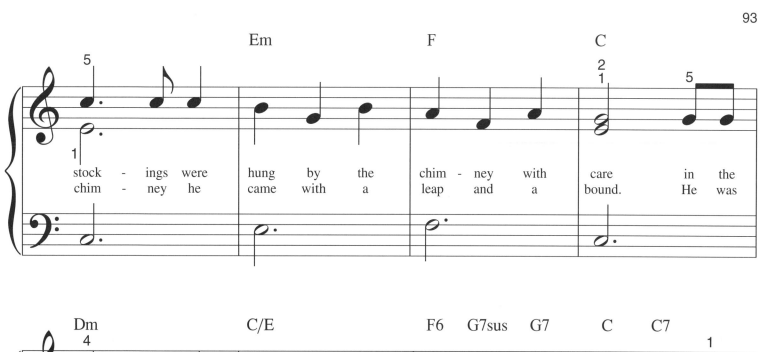

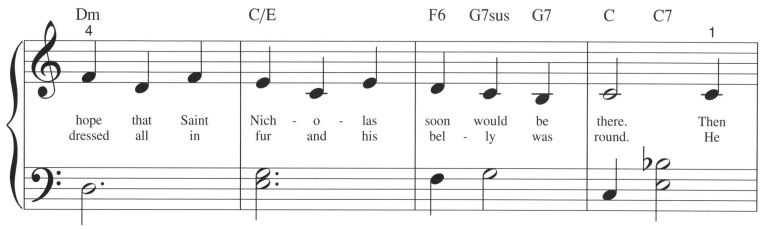

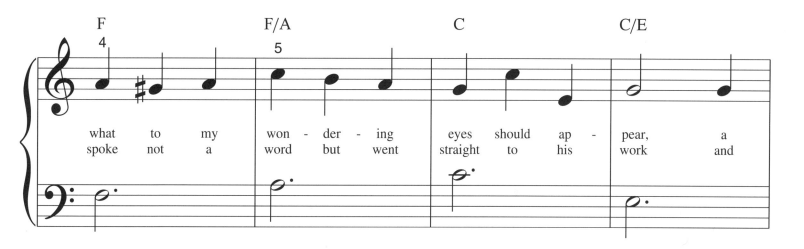

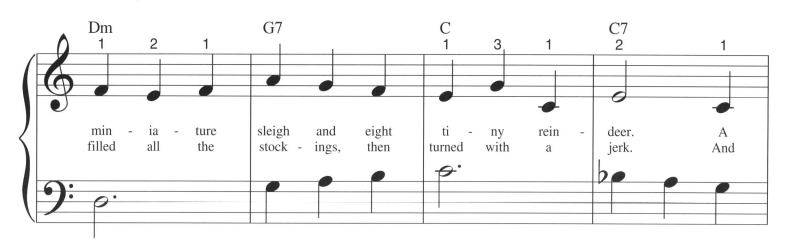

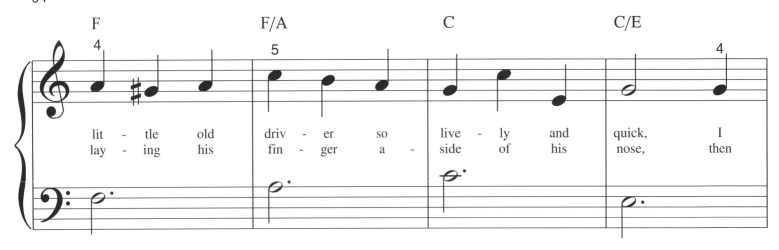

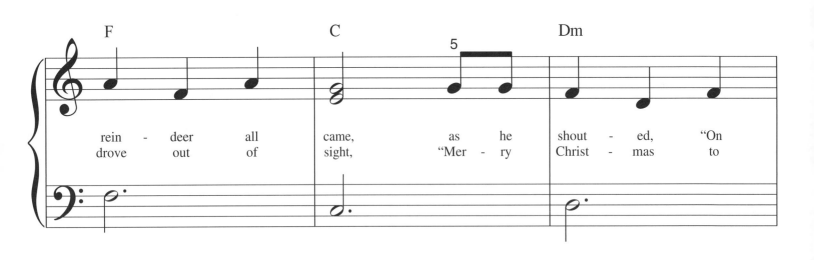

ROCKIN' AROUND THE CHRISTMAS TREE

Music and Lyrics by
JOHNNY MARKS

RUDOLPH THE RED-NOSED REINDEER

Music and Lyrics by
JOHNNY MARKS

100

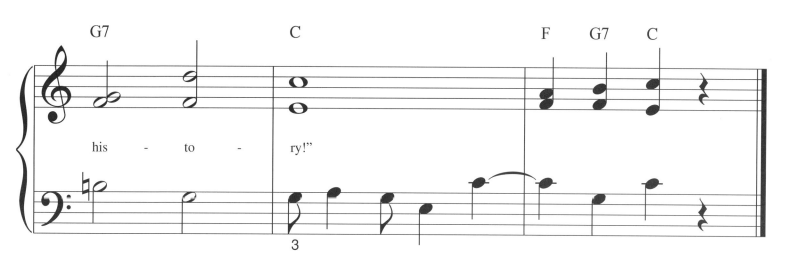

Silver Bells
from the Paramount Picture THE LEMON DROP KID

Words and Music by JAY LIVINGSTON
and RAY EVANS

SUZY SNOWFLAKE

Words and Music by SID TEPPER
and ROY BENNETT

WE NEED A LITTLE CHRISTMAS

from MAME

Music and Lyric by
JERRY HERMAN

Haul out the hol - ly,_____ put up the
climb down the chim - ney,_____ turn on the

tree be - fore my spir - it falls_____ a - gain.
bright - est string of lights I've ev - er seen.

Fill up the stock - ing, I may be
Slice up the fruit - cake, it's time we

rush - ing things, but deck the halls_____ a - gain
hung some tin - sel on the ev - er - green

CELEBRATE THE SEASON
with Christmas Songbooks for Piano from Hal Leonard

17 Super Christmas Hits

This book contains the most popular, most requested Christmas titles: The Christmas Song • Frosty the Snow Man • A Holly Jolly Christmas • Home for the Holidays • I'll Be Home for Christmas • It's Beginning to Look like Christmas • Jingle-Bell Rock • Let It Snow! Let It Snow! Let It Snow! • The Little Drummer Boy • Mister Santa • Sleigh Ride • We Need a Little Christmas • and more.
00240867 Big-Note Piano $9.95
00361053 Easy Piano $9.95

25 Top Christmas Songs

Includes: Blue Christmas • C-H-R-I-S-T-M-A-S • The Christmas Song • The Christmas Waltz • Do You Hear What I Hear • Have Yourself a Merry Little Christmas • Here Comes Santa Claus • Jingle-Bell Rock • Last Christmas • Pretty Paper • Silver Bells • and more.
00290064 Big-Note Piano $9.95
00490058 Easy Piano $10.95

Best Christmas Music

A giant collection of 62 Christmas favorites: Away in a Manger • Blue Christmas • The Chipmunk Song • The First Noel • Frosty the Snow Man • Grandma Got Run Over by a Reindeer • I Saw Mommy Kissing Santa Claus • Pretty Paper • Silver Bells • Wonderful Christmastime • more.
00310325 Big-Note Piano $14.95

The Best Christmas Songs Ever

A treasured collection of 70 songs: The Christmas Song • Frosty the Snow Man • Grandma Got Run Over by a Reindeer • Here Comes Santa Claus • A Holly Jolly Christmas • I'll Be Home for Christmas • Jingle-Bell Rock • Let It Snow! Let It Snow! Let It Snow! • Santa Claus Is Comin' to Town • more!
00364130 Easy Piano $18.95

Children's Christmas Songs

22 holiday favorites, including: Frosty the Snow Man • Jingle Bells • Jolly Old St. Nicholas • Rudolph, the Red-Nosed Reindeer • Up on the Housetop • and more!
00222547 Easy Piano $7.95

Christmas Pops
THE PHILLIP KEVEREN SERIES

18 holiday favorites: Because It's Christmas • Blue Christmas • Christmas Time Is Here • I'll Be Home for Christmas • Mary, Did You Know? • Rockin' Around the Christmas Tree • Silver Bells • Tennessee Christmas • more.
00311126 Easy Piano $12.95

Christmas Songs

12 songs, including: Caroling, Caroling • Christmas Time Is Here • Do You Hear What I Hear • Here Comes Santa Claus • It's Beginning to Look like Christmas • Little Saint Nick • Merry Christmas, Darling • Mistletoe and Holly • and more.
00311242 Easy Piano Solo...........................$8.95

Christmas Traditions
THE PHILLIP KEVEREN SERIES

20 beloved songs arranged for beginning soloists: Away in a Manger • Coventry Carol • Deck the Hall • God Rest Ye Merry, Gentlemen • Jingle Bells • Silent Night • We Three Kings of Orient Are • more.
00311117 Beginning Piano Solos...................$9.95

Greatest Christmas Hits

18 Christmas classics: Blue Christmas • Brazilian Sleigh Bells • The Christmas Song • Do You Hear What I Hear • Here Comes Santa Claus • I Saw Mommy Kissing Santa Claus • Silver Bells • This Christmas • more!
00311136 Big-Note Piano $9.95

Jazz Up Your Christmas
ARRANGED BY LEE EVANS

12 Christmas carols in a fresh perspective. Full arrangements may be played as a concert suite. Songs include: Deck the Hall • The First Noel • God Rest Ye Merry Gentlemen • The Holly and the Ivy • O Christmas Tree • What Child Is This? • and more.
00009040 Piano Solo $7.95

Jingle Jazz
THE PHILLIP KEVEREN SERIES

17 Christmas standards: Caroling, Caroling • The Christmas Song • I'll Be Home for Christmas • Jingle Bells • Merry Christmas, Darling • The Most Wonderful Time of the Year • Rudolph the Red-Nosed Reindeer • We Wish You a Merry Christmas • and more.
00310762 Piano Solo $12.95

100 Christmas Carols

Includes the Christmas classics: Angels We Have Heard on High • Bring a Torch, Jeannette Isabella • Dance of the Sugar Plum Fairy • The First Noel • Here We Come A-Wassailing • It Came upon the Midnight Clear • Joy to the World • Still, Still, Still • The Twelve Days of Christmas • We Three Kings of Orient Are • and more!
00311134 Easy Piano................................$14.95

The Nutcracker Suite
ARRANGED BY BILL BOYD

7 easy piano arrangements from Tchaikovsky's beloved ballet. Includes "Dance of the Sugar-Plum Fairy."
00110010 Easy Piano.................................$8.95

The Ultimate Series: Christmas

The ultimate collection of Christmas classics includes 100 songs: Carol of the Bells • The Chipmunk Song • Christmas Time Is Here • Do You Hear What I Hear • The First Noel • Gesù Bambino • Happy Xmas (War Is Over) • Jesu, Joy of Man's Desiring • Silver and Gold • What Child Is This? • Wonderful Christmastime • and more.
00241003 Easy Piano................................$19.95

FOR MORE INFORMATION, SEE YOUR LOCAL MUSIC DEALER, OR WRITE TO:

HAL•LEONARD® CORPORATION
7777 W. BLUEMOUND RD. P.O. BOX 13819 MILWAUKEE, WI 53213
Complete songlists online at **www.halleonard.com**

Prices, contents and availability subject to change without notice.